Let's Throw a

Hanukkah Party!

Rachel Lynette

PowerKiDS press

New York

For my mom, who throws the very best Hanukkah parties!

Published in 2012 by The Rosen Publishing Group, Inc.
29 East 21st Street, New York, NY 10010

First Edition

Editor: Joanne Randolph
Layout Design: Greg Tucker

Photo Credits: Cover (main) Jupiterimages/Photos.com/Thinkstock; cover (dreidel), pp. 4–5, 10, 17 (middle), 17 (bottom), 19, 21 Shutterstock.com; pp. 6–7 Judas Maccabeus at Maspha, illustration from L'Ancien Testament, published by Jakob Ferdinand Schreiber, Esslingen (color engraving), German School (19th century)/Bibliotheque des Arts Decoratifs, Paris, France/The Bridgeman Art Library International; p. 9 Jupiterimages/Pixland/Thinkstock; p. 11 © www.iStockphoto.com/Nick M. Do; p. 12 Bushnell/Soifer/Getty Images; p. 13 © www.iStockphoto.com/Amit Erez; p. 14 Hemera/Thinkstock; p. 15 (bottom) Barry Wong/Getty Images; p. 18 Stephen Chernin/Getty Images; p. 22 Daniel Mihailescu/AFP/Getty Images.

Library of Congress Cataloging-in-Publication Data

Lynette, Rachel.
 Let's throw a Hanukkah party! / by Rachel Lynette. — 1st ed.
     p. cm. — (Holiday parties)
 Includes index.
 ISBN 978-1-4488-2572-1 (library binding) — ISBN 978-1-4488-2733-6 (pbk.) —
ISBN 978-1-4488-2734-3 (6-pack)
 1. Hanukkah decorations—Juvenile literature. 2. Hanukkah cooking—Juvenile literature. 3. Children's parties—Juvenile literature.. I. Title.
 TT900.H34L96 2012
 745.594'1—dc22

                              2010032132

Manufactured in the United States of America

CPSIA Compliance Information: Batch #WW11PK: For Further Information contact Rosen Publishing, New York, New York at 1-800-237-9932

Contents

Eight Days to Celebrate!

Hanukkah is a special holiday for Jewish people. Hanukkah is generally **celebrated** in December. Hanukkah lasts for eight days! Each evening, Jewish families light candles in a special candleholder, called a **menorah**.

It is a Jewish law to spread the word about Hanukkah by lighting a menorah. It should be lit at sundown with the whole family present. The menorah is then put outside or in a window, when possible, where more people will see it.

Children often receive a present each night. Families eat special foods, such as potato pancakes called **latkes**. They read Hanukkah stories and play a game called **dreidel**.

People also go to Hanukkah parties to celebrate with friends. There are many fun things to do at a Hanukkah party. This book will give you ideas about how you can throw a Hanukkah party of your own!

The Miracle of Hanukkah

Jewish people celebrate Hanukkah because of a **miracle** that happened thousands of years ago in Israel. At that time the Greek king had outlawed Judaism. The Greek army took over the Jewish **temple**. Jewish soldiers called the Maccabees fought against the Greek army and won.

The Jews took their temple back and cleaned it. The temple was **rededicated** to

To honor the miracle of the oil, Jews celebrate Hanukkah for eight days each year. The word "hanukkah" means "dedication."

God. Jewish temples must have a lamp burning in them each night. However, there was only enough oil for the fire to be lit for one night. It would take eight days for new holy oil to be made. Then a miracle happened. The lamp burned for eight days!

Plan Your Party

YOU ARE INVITED TO A
HANUKKAH PARTY!
WHEN: DECEMBER 7 AT 3PM
WHERE: MY HOUSE
FROM: SARA

Try This!

To make your own invitations, cut dreidel shapes out of blue paper. Cut and glue a rectangle of white paper on top of your dreidel shape. Write your party information on it and decorate the invitation. Now you are ready to put them in envelopes and mail them!

You can plan your party for any of the eight days of Hanukkah. You will want to make a list of all the guests you want to **invite**. Be sure to send your invitations out at least two weeks before the big day.

You will also want to make a list of the things you will need for your party. Your list should include the **decorations** you will need. It should include the food you will serve, too. You will also want to think about what you will need for party activities, such as games and crafts. You may want to run your party plans by an adult, too.

It is fun to make Hanukkah decorations! The traditional colors of Hanukkah are blue, white, gold, and silver. Hanukkah decorations are often shaped like dreidels, menorahs, and **Stars of David**. For large decorations to hang on the wall, try cutting Hanukkah shapes from wrapping paper.

Left: Blue and gold ribbon can be hung like streamers around the party room. *Above:* Party stores may have small dreidels, foil-wrapped gold coins called gelt, and serving bowls in fun Hanukkah shapes.

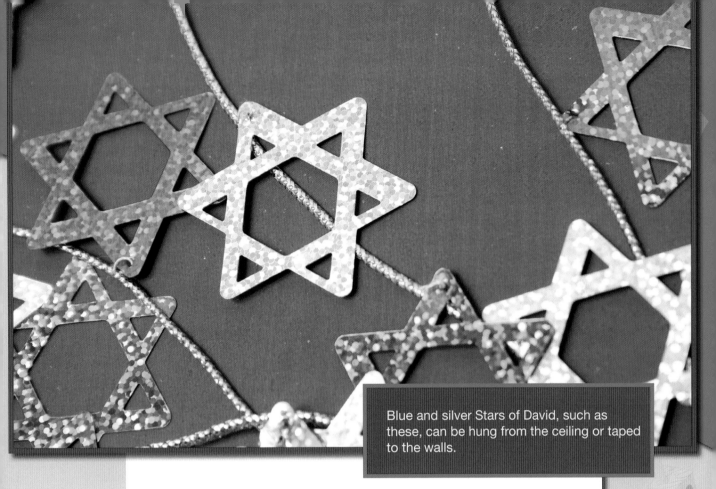

Blue and silver Stars of David, such as these, can be hung from the ceiling or taped to the walls.

You may also want to make a banner for your party. You can make your banner on a long piece of paper and color it with Hanukkah colors. You could also make dreidel cutouts and put one letter on each cutout. Tape the cutouts to a long piece of string to spell out the words "Happy Hanukkah." Use glitter to make your banner sparkle!

A menorah is a special candleholder that is used only on Hanukkah. It has holders for nine candles. Eight of the candles are for the eight days of Hanukkah. The ninth candle is the helper candle. It is called the *shamash*. It is used to light the other candles.

On each night of Hanukkah, a new candle is added to the menorah. On

The menorah is also called the *hanukiah*. Blessings are said each night before lighting the candles. Songs are often sung after the candles are lit, too.

You can make your own menorah with small pieces of wood that you can buy in a hardware or craft store. Paint 10 small blocks of wood any colors you like. Then glue them in a row to a piece of wood. Glue a second block to the one in the center to make a holder for the shamash. Use metal nuts or silver rings to hold the candles.

the first night, there should be one candle on the far right side of the menorah. Use the shamash to light that candle and leave both candles burning. On the second night, light the shamash and two candles. The menorah will not be lit with all nine candles until the last night of Hanukkah.

Tasty Hanukkah Treats

You might want to serve some traditional Hanukkah foods at your party. People often make food that is fried in oil to celebrate the miracle of the oil that lasted for eight days. Latkes are a favorite Hanukkah treat. Latkes are fried potato pancakes. Latkes are often served with applesauce or sour cream.

Sufganiyot are another food that people eat during Hanukkah. Sufganiyot are like jelly doughnuts that are fried in oil and then dipped in powdered sugar or cinnamon.

This girl gets ready to eat her sufganiyah. Jewish bakeries make thousands of sufganiyot as Hanukkah gets closer.

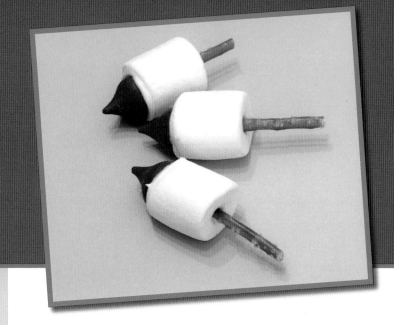

Try This!

You can make treats in the shape of dreidels. Just use white frosting to stick a chocolate kiss to one end of a marshmallow. Push a pretzel stick into the other end.

Hanukkah gelt is another treat that children enjoy at Hanukkah. Hanukkah gelt are chocolate coins wrapped in gold foil. Small bags of gelt make a nice party favor for your guests!

Sugar cookies in Hanukkah shapes are fun to make and yummy to eat, too!

Let's Make Latkes

Latkes are not hard to make. You will need an adult to help, though. This recipe makes about 20 pancakes.

What you need:

6 potatoes
1 small onion
2 eggs
1 teaspoon salt
2 to 4 tablespoons flour
Oil
Colander or strainer
Large bowl
Frying pan
Potato peeler
Cheese grater

What you do:

1

Peel the potatoes and grate them into a colander. Use your hands to squish the extra water out of the potatoes. Then put them in a big bowl.

2

Grate the onion and add it to the potatoes.

16

3

Beat the eggs and add them, too.

4

Then add the salt and enough flour to absorb the extra liquid. Mix it all together.

5

Heat about 1/4 inch (6 mm) of oil in a frying pan.

6

Drop tablespoons of the batter into the oil. Brown the pancakes until the edges are crispy. Then turn them over to brown the other sides.

7

Put the cooked pancakes on a paper towel to get rid of the extra oil. Serve hot with sour cream or applesauce.

Spin the Dreidel

Dreidel is a game that is played with a special spinning top. The top has four letters on it. To play, give everyone the same number of small items such as peanuts, raisins, gelt, or pennies. To start, everyone puts one item in the center. Then players take turns spinning the dreidel.

Here children are playing dreidel. Back when Judaism was outlawed, Jews secretly taught each other from a religious book, called the Torah. They kept dreidels with them. When Greek guards passed them, they hid the Torah and played with the top!

Each of the four letters on the dreidel stands for a different Hebrew word. Together, the words say, "A great miracle happened here."

The letter that lands face up tells the player what to do. If the dreidel lands on *nun*, the player does nothing. If it lands on *shin*, the player must put another item into the center. If it lands on *hay*, the player takes half the pile. If it lands on *gimmel*, the player takes the whole pile.

Make a Star of David

You might want to plan to make a craft at your Hanukkah party. The Star of David is an important Jewish **symbol**. Your guests can make their own Stars of David from craft sticks. You will need glue and six craft sticks for each star. First, glue three craft sticks into a triangle. Then glue three more

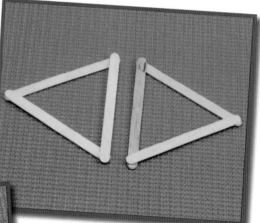

sticks into another triangle. Let the glue dry, then glue the triangles together to make a star shape.

Your guests can paint their stars blue and gold. They can decorate them with buttons, sequins, beads, or glitter. When they are dry, tie a piece of string to one of the points and hang the stars in the window.

More Ways to Celebrate

One fun thing to do on Hanukkah is to act out the story of the Hanukkah miracle. Split your guests into two groups. Give the groups a few minutes to practice acting out the story. One

> Some favorite Hanukkah songs are "Hanukkah Oh Hanukkah" and "I Have a Little Dreidel."

group can act out the story first while the other group is the audience, then switch.

It is also fun to sing Hanukkah songs. Some Hanukkah songs are in **Hebrew** while others are in English. If your guests do not know a song, you can teach it to them! During the party, you can ask guests for ideas for next year's Hanukkah party!

Glossary

celebrated (SEH-luh-brayt-ed) Honored an important moment by doing special things.

decorations (deh-kuh-RAY-shunz) Objects that make things prettier.

dreidel (DRAY-dul) A four-sided top with one Hebrew letter on each side, used to play a Hanukkah game. The game is also called dreidel.

Hebrew (HEE-broo) A language spoken in Israel and throughout the world.

invite (in-VYT) To ask people if they will come to a party.

latkes (LAHT-keez) Potato pancakes that are fried in oil and often eaten during Hanukkah.

menorah (meh-NOR-uh) A candleholder with nine candles, used in the Hanukkah celebration.

miracle (MEER-uh-kul) A wonderful or an unexpected event said to have been done by God.

rededicated (ree-DEH-dih-kayt-ed) Set apart for a special use again.

Stars of David (STAHRZ UV DAY-vud) Six-pointed stars that are used to stand for the Jewish faith.

sufganiyot (soof-gah-nee-YOHT) Jelly-filled pastries that are fried in oil and eaten during Hanukkah.

symbol (SIM-bul) An object or a picture that stands for something else.

temple (TEM-pul) A place where people go to worship.

Index

Web Sites

Due to the changing nature of Internet links, PowerKids Press has developed an online list of Web sites related to the subject of this book. This site is updated regularly. Please use this link to access the list:
www.powerkidslinks.com/hp/hanukkah/